If I forget thee, O Jerusalem,

let my right hand forget her cunning.

If I do not remember thee,

let my tongue cleave to the roof of my mouth;

if I prefer not Jerusalem above my chief joy.

PSALM OF DAVID 137

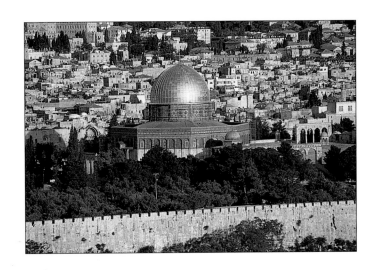

If I Forget Thee,
O JERUSALEM

WRITTEN AND PHOTOGRAPHED BY BERNARD WOLF

DUTTON CHILDREN'S BOOKS · NEW YORK

ACKNOWLEDGMENTS

I wish to thank the following people for their assistance in the preparation of this book:
Zvi Greenhut, Director of Information and Education, Israel Antiquities Authority; Ya-akov Billig, Archaeologist,
Israel Antiquities Authority; Adnan Husseini, General Director of the Muslim Council, Jerusalem; and my editor, Lucia Monfried,
Dutton Children's Books. Finally, I am indebted to Laurin Lucaire, Dutton Children's Books,
for her perceptive and superb design of this book. Many, many thanks!

COPYRIGHT © 1998 BY BERNARD WOLF
ALL RIGHTS RESERVED.

Library of Congress Cataloging-in-Publication Data

Wolf, Bernard, date.
If I forget Thee, O Jerusalem/written and photographed by Bernard Wolf.—1st ed. p. cm.
Summary: Surveys the history of the city of Jerusalem and its importance to
three of the world's major religions: Judaism, Christianity, and Islam.
ISBN 0-525-45738-0 (hardcover)
I. Jerusalem—History—Juvenile literature. [1. Jerusalem—History] I. Title.
DS109.9.W65 1998 956.94'42—DC21 98-11106 CIP AC

PUBLISHED IN THE UNITED STATES 1998
BY DUTTON CHILDREN'S BOOKS,
A MEMBER OF PENGUIN PUTNAM INC.
375 HUDSON STREET, NEW YORK, NEW YORK 10014
DESIGNED BY LAURIN LUCAIRE
PRINTED IN HONG KONG · FIRST EDITION
1 3 5 7 9 10 8 6 4 2

W HO, IN THEIR WILDEST IMAGININGS, could ever have foreseen
that this dusty, sunbaked place with its unimpressive hills was
destined to become the fountain from which sprang the world's three
greatest faiths: Judaism, Christianity, and Islam? This place that has,
to this day, witnessed more devotion, inspiration, destruction, and
bloodshed than any other on earth? This little place called Jerusalem.

In 1000 B.C., King David led his warriors here to a small, high-
walled hilltop town called Jebus, after its inhabitants, the Jebusites,
who were a fierce, pagan people. David captured the town and
renamed it Jerusalem. He had important plans for this site.

David had recently won an astonishing victory over the dreaded
Philistines, which had ensured his people's very survival in this
"promised land." That victory, plus his fame as a singer, harpist, and
poet, drew many followers to him. But David was also a brilliant
politician. These were the skills he now needed.

The people David ruled called themselves Israelites. In their
Hebrew language, this meant "the champions of God," who were
descended from Abraham, Isaac, and Jacob.

The Israelites were a nomadic people, divided into twelve tribes, each protective of its own importance and constantly quarreling with the others. Ten of the tribes who settled in the north called this land Israel. The two remaining tribes who settled in the south referred to it as Judah.

David needed a new, neutral capital from where he could govern and unite all the tribes into one single nation. This "Jerusalem," in the center of the land, would be the ideal spot. Here he would build a great city on a ridge between two valleys, with a steep hillside below, which could be easily defended from behind thick, high walls.

David had another, equally urgent plan for this place. He was a man totally devoted to Yahweh, the sole, invisible, but all-powerful God of the Israelites. David even claimed that he spoke directly to him. David's warriors had brought to Jerusalem the Holy of Holies, the Ark of the Covenant, a gold-covered wooden casket enclosing the stone tablets on which were engraved the Ten Commandments given by Yahweh to Moses. It represented the most sacred foundation and proof of his people's faith in their God. Now, David planned to build a magnificent temple to house the Ark of the Covenant. Thus, he would achieve two goals. Not only would his Jerusalem become the center of government for all the tribes of Israel, but it would also unite them here as their spiritual center as well.

On Mount Moriah, the highest hill above David's new city, there was a large level area owned by a Jebusite woman who used it as a threshing floor. David purchased this space. Here, on this Temple Mount, he planned to build the Holy House of God. But David was forbidden this task by Yahweh. David was a man of war. The Temple must be dedicated to peace. It was constructed after David's death by his son, King Solomon.

And so, this place that began with but three thousand souls, became, with its Temple, unto this very day, a magnet for the world. This little place called Jerusalem.

Solomon's Temple filled all who saw it with awe. Beyond its magnificent altar, in a dark, sealed chamber, lay the Ark of the Covenant. Word spread through the land that Jerusalem had been selected by Yahweh as his eternal dwelling place. Just as David had planned, Jerusalem was established as the spiritual and political capital of the Israelites.

Thanks to his father's conquests, King Solomon now ruled an impressive empire five times the size of modern Israel. Shrewdly, Solomon made new treaties with his nation's enemies, thus ensuring peace. And in that peace, he changed forever the Israelites' way of life from nomads who lived in tents, to farmers, city dwellers, craftsmen, ship builders, and merchants. And the people prospered.

Those were the glory years of the Israelites. But after Solomon's death, the old rivalries erupted once more between the tribes of the north and the south. The nation broke into two kingdoms: Israel in the north and Judah, with Jerusalem as its capital, in the south.

The separate kingdoms fought among themselves for political power. They also fought against increasingly bolder foreign neighbors to retain control of valuable trade routes. One of those neighbors was a fierce new kingdom called Assyria. Emerging in the east, Assyria sought access to seaports for its ships but Israel stood in the way.

In 722 B.C., after many onslaughts, the Assyrians conquered Northern Israel, sending all those Israelites who survived slaughter to far-off Mesopotamia. They were never heard from again. Now, only the kingdom of Judah remained of what was once the single, mighty empire of King Solomon.

During the battles with the Assyrians, many Israelites had fled south to Jerusalem for asylum. By now, the city had grown from a mere 27 acres to 150 acres in size. Fortified Jerusalem withstood repeated attacks by the Assyrians, who were also engaged in conflict with their own neighbors, and with the Babylonians, a rising power.

In 586 B.C., the Babylonians, under King Nebuchadnezzar, breached the walls of Jerusalem and laid waste to the Holy City. They destroyed Solomon's Temple—the Holy House of God. The Ark of the Covenant vanished, never to be rediscovered. Most of the people of Judah were sent to Babylon as captives and slaves. After more than four hundred years, the independent Israelite-Judean state was no more.

All empires rise only to one day yield their glory to others. So it was with Babylon. While the exiled people of Israel wept for Jerusalem, Babylon was captured by King Cyrus of the Persians in 540 B.C. Cyrus was a great warrior, but also a man of sense who saw no reason to destroy useful cities or their inhabitants unnecessarily. Babylon fell with hardly a murmur.

The Babylonians had not treated their captive Judeans harshly. Some were given positions of importance in the royal court. Others engaged in commerce and grew prosperous. But most longed to return to their homeland.

Around 537 B.C., Cyrus issued a decree allowing those Jews (as they were now identified) who so desired to return to Judah and rebuild their Temple in Jerusalem. Twenty-one years later, a second Temple sat atop Mount Moriah, rededicated to Yahweh and to peace. Nevertheless, the Jews now lived under Persian rule.

Then, in 332 B.C., after a stunning victory over the Persians, Alexander the Great marched triumphantly into Jerusalem and annexed Judea as an addition to his expanding Greek Empire. It was a peaceful takeover. Alexander granted the Jews internal political and religious freedom. He also introduced the Jews to Greek art, architecture, philosophy, and ordered his officers and men to intermarry with the native women and beget many Greek children.

But upon Alexander's untimely death at the age of thirty-two, his generals fought each other for a piece of his empire. In the following power struggle, Jerusalem was occupied and ruled by the Ptolemies of Egypt. Now, the Orthodox Jews and priests of the Temple began to openly express their outrage over the corruption of their youth by the pagan Greeks, and unrest spread through the land.

Meanwhile, a new empire, destined to become the mightiest of the ancient world, had begun its march of conquest—Rome! In 63 B.C., following a three-month siege of Jerusalem, a Roman army broke through the walls of Mount Moriah, slaughtering twelve thousand defending Jews, and entered the Temple itself. With this victory, the new masters of the Jews established Roman civil law, leaving in Jerusalem Roman governors to preside over their courts, and garrisons of Roman soldiers to enforce their laws and keep the peace. They constructed the "cardo," a broad, columned thoroughfare in the city, to bring in soldiers and goods.

During the next twenty years, a strange, shrewd, and ambitious man called Herod emerged. He was a half-Jew who proved his loyalty to the Romans by ruthlessly putting down the Jewish rebellion in the land the Romans called Judea. In later years they renamed it Palestina, or Palestine. In return, the Romans appointed Herod king over the Jews, many of whom feared, despised, and mistrusted him. Herod was a suspicious man who, in fits of mad rage, had any suspected rivals for his power put to death, including two of his wives and three of his sons. In spite of this, the thirty-three years of his reign proved a remarkably stable and prosperous period.

But Herod's greatest achievements lay in his genius as a master builder. In 20 B.C., he turned these talents toward Jerusalem. Jerusalem had grown to many times the size of King Solomon's city. Its inhabitants now numbered in the hundreds of thousands. It was one of the world's largest cities and attracted many pilgrims. Herod began a monumental program of enlargement and beautification of Jerusalem. A model of Herod's city as it looked in his time can be seen in Jerusalem today.

In the Roman style, he built and enlarged markets for the populace. He built a theater, amphitheater, and a stadium for chariot races and other spectator events. He constructed imposing government buildings. He built huge, luxurious palaces for himself, Roman officials, and for the high priest of the Temple.

For his primary building material, Herod used what was most readily at hand: Jerusalem's own, native limestone. Tunnels and caverns were carved into the hills of the city. There, great white blocks of stone were quarried, cut, and transported to their various destinations. It was a mammoth undertaking. The Jewish historian Josephus called it, "the most prodigious work that was ever heard of by man."

Above all, Herod lavished his major effort on the Temple Mount and the Temple itself. This would be the crowning glory of his city, the spiritual heart and soul of the Jewish people, the place that identified them as God's chosen people for all time. It would be a wonder to the world. It would also ensure Herod his place in history.

Herod enlarged the enormous, paved platform upon which the Temple stood to twice its original size, from twenty to forty acres. In order to support this expansion, he completely surrounded it with massive stone walls. At its highest point, one wall rose 211 feet from its base. At the top, a trumpeting priest would signal the beginning of the Sabbath to the city's Jews.

Near the southwest corner of the Western Wall, he constructed a great, arched stairway leading to the gates into the Temple Mount platform. Beneath this ran a long, paved concourse lined with shops where religious objects were sold and where silversmiths and goldsmiths pursued their crafts.

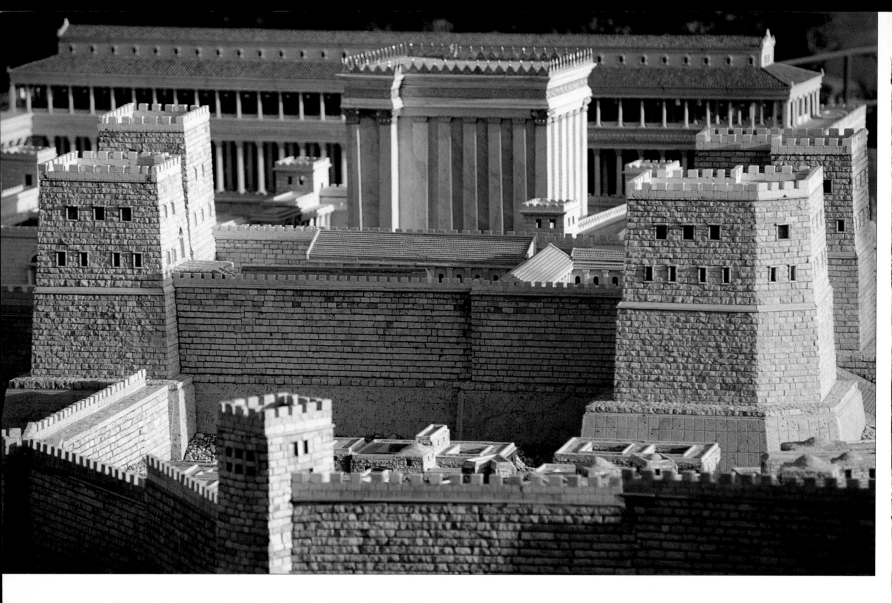

Ever a vigilant man, Herod built on the northern side of the
mount the Antonia Fortress, named in honor of his Roman friend,
Marc Antony. The fortress was cornered by four high towers over-
looking the entire Temple complex with its many elaborate court-
yards, chapels, and its sacrificial altar. From here, a rebellion
could quickly be dealt with by the Roman garrison.

Finally, there was the supreme reason for Herod's titanic building program: the "sacred House of God," the Temple. Herod proceeded to remodel, beautify, and enlarge the structure, though he was careful not to alter Solomon's original proportions. The work was done by a thousand priests who were trained as masons, carpenters, and artisans. No unclean hands were permitted these tasks.

The sanctuary's interior was narrow, dim, and heavy with the smoke of the great seven-branched menorah and burnt incense.

Beyond lay a dark, empty chamber—the Holy of Holies, a place of mystery and power.

Outside, the Temple soared to a height of 150 feet, crowned with a golden, spiked gallery to keep birds from soiling the facade. The enormous portal of the structure was an entrance of layers of stone and wood sixty-six feet high and thirty-three feet wide. The entire exterior was covered by white marble and richly decorated with gold. From a distance, the whole Temple resembled "a snowy mountain glittering in the sun," according to Josephus.

Herod did not live to see the completion of all his works. He died in 4 B.C., riddled by disease and madness. The Temple was not finished until A.D. 64, sixty-eight years later.

After Herod's death, corrupt and incompetent Roman procurators were sent to Palestine. These were high officials whose main tasks were collecting taxes and keeping the peace. They regarded the Jews as an inferior and troublesome people. There was great resentment against Roman taxation and brutality in the land.

In A.D. 66, the enraged Jews of Jerusalem rose in armed revolt against their oppressors and slew the city's Roman garrison. The bloody uprising spread far beyond Jerusalem. Rome was slow to respond, but when it did, what followed was the greatest disaster yet experienced by the Jews.

In A.D. 70, a huge Roman army led by Titus, the son of Rome's emperor, battered down the outer ramparts and second walls of Jerusalem. The defending Jews retreated behind the heavy fortifications of the Temple Mount. Titus decided to starve them out. As the siege progressed, desperate citizens slipped through the gates of the inner city, searching for grass and roots to eat. Most were caught and crucified by the Romans, sometimes as many as five hundred each day.

After a month, the Romans captured the Antonia Fortress. The Jews retreated farther behind the walls of the Temple's outer court. They fought fiercely for another month. The Romans finally set fire to the gates and broke through to the inner court and then to the sanctuary. Impressed by the Temple's magnificence, Titus commanded that it not be damaged. But it was too late. His soldiers, maddened by bloodlust, were beyond control. The great doors of the Temple were set ablaze. Quickly, the structure was engulfed in flame, and the Holy House of God destroyed.

As the victor, Titus could now claim Jerusalem for Rome. But when he was told that a starving Jewish mother had roasted and eaten her own child, he ordered that the entire city be razed to the ground. By fire and by brute strength, the Romans reduced the city to rubble. The stones of the Temple were battered down and hurled over its supporting walls.

The Temple, completed only six years earlier, was no more. And Jerusalem, the "city of peace," was no more.

Jerusalem lay in ruins until A.D. 135, when the emperor Hadrian ordered a new, Roman city built on the site. He called it Aelia Capitolina. But in the centuries that followed, violence and bloodshed revisited this place. In A.D. 614, Jerusalem was invaded and destroyed by the Persians. In A.D. 638, the city was conquered by Arab forces and for the next 325 years, all of Palestine came under Muslim domination. In A.D. 1099, the first wave of Crusaders arrived to claim the holy places for Christianity. They conquered Jerusalem, taking it from the Arabs only to lose it to them in A.D. 1187. In A.D. 1261, Jerusalem fell to the Mamluks of Egypt, who controlled it until 1517, when it was taken and held by the Turks for 400 years. In 1917, Jerusalem and all of Palestine came under British rule.

Each new conqueror built his own city atop the ruins of the Jerusalem that was here before, or added to what had survived destruction. Pagan temples, mosques, churches, palaces, and new fortifications were constructed, changing the style and shape of the city over time. Some of these structures have survived the ages.

After a desperate battle in 1967, the Jews reclaimed the Old City of Jerusalem from the Arabs, declaring it part of modern Israel's "eternal capital." Now they were finally able to begin excavations into their own ancient history.

At the end of the nineteenth century, the only original remnant of the second Temple of the Jews was its western retaining wall, built by Herod to support his expansion of the Temple's platform. Most of this wall's long, southern extension was covered by high hills of hard-packed earth, which had accumulated over many centuries.

In 1968, a team of Israeli archaeologists undertook the most important excavations in all of Israel. They concentrated their efforts around the southern and western base of the Temple Mount, hoping to discover what, if anything, remained of Herod's ancient city. The archaeologists peeled away the layers of Jerusalem's past, digging through the Mamluk, Crusader, Islamic, and Roman periods and finding many artifacts from each. Then, at the southern base of the mount, after years of careful labor, they made a dramatic discovery! They uncovered the great stone stairway that had led up to the two major gates into the Temple Mount. These were the very steps Jesus ascended some 2,000 years ago.

In 1980, the work of those first archaeologists stopped, leaving excavations along the southern stretch of the Western Wall unfinished. But in 1994, a new expedition arrived to complete the work begun earlier. And what they have found has excited archaeologists, historians, and scholars alike; they have discovered Herod's grand shopping arcade, just as it was described by ancient historians! A few of the shops' doorframes still stand along one side and half of the large, original paving stones of the broad concourse have been laid bare. Now, the archaeologists are digging through the remaining thirteen feet of packed earth and rubble to uncover the other half of the street buried next to the base of the Western Wall.

Here, the ancient stones of the wall rise to about 67 feet. In Herod's time, the wall was at least twice that height. The average Herodian stone used in its construction weighs two to ten tons. But the largest weigh as much as 415 tons and measure ten feet high and wide, and 46 feet in length! No mortar was used in the construction of the wall. Herod's masons fitted them together so perfectly that not even a knife's blade may pass between them! Archaeologists and engineers have long puzzled over this. Even with the most modern machines and technology currently available, it is nearly impossible to grasp how these gigantic stones were moved to their destinations and so precisely set in place.

The northern part of the street is heaped with the battered stones of the Temple, shoved down by the Romans long ago. These will not be disturbed. They will remain where they fell in remembrance of the Temple's destruction.

A small shaft has been sunk deep beneath the paving stones of Herod's street. Using a winch, buckets of earth are lifted up, then carefully sifted in a search for artifacts from Herod's time and from earlier periods.

Nearby, at the expedition's field office, the artifacts that have been found are laid out for examination: bits of pottery, carved stone fragments, clay oil lamps, parts of containers for liquids, and ancient coins.

So far, most of the coins found have been two-thousand-year-old Jewish bronze pennies called *agarot*, heavily crusted by earth and corrosion. Coins are important because they confirm specific dates from the past. But shards of pottery are equally informative. The fragments pried from each layer of earth reveal much about the people who made these objects. From their designs and how they were left unglazed or glazed and fired, scientists can learn who their makers were, where they came from, and when they formed a part of Jerusalem's history.

The artifacts are washed and scrubbed clean. When they are dry, each fragment is carefully cataloged according to description and the measured depth of earth in which it was uncovered. They are inscribed with inked identification numbers and filed for further study. It is slow and meticulous work.

On an early summer afternoon, a large group of Israeli and foreign dignitaries are taken on a guided tour of the excavation site. As they marvel at what the archaeologists have accomplished, high above their heads on the Western Wall, a line of stones can be seen protruding from its surface. These stones are the basis of another major discovery.

In the 1830s, an American explorer named Edward Robinson noticed, near the Western Wall's southern corner, barely visible above the mounds of earth covering most of it, a line of stones that slanted out at an angle from the wall's otherwise flat surface. He deduced that these stones must have been the top of a great arched stairway. When the entire Western Wall was later uncovered, archaeologists could plainly see that there had been an arch here and named it after its discoverer. They also determined that Robinson's Arch was the last of a series of arches that formed a monumental stairway soaring from the far side of the street below, up to a gate into the Temple Mount!

These excavations are not open to the public now, but when the project is completed, new staircases with safety rails will be installed. Then, everyone will be welcome to view the mighty works of Herod the Great. Meanwhile, if, after digging down to the bottom of the wall, a stone should be uncovered that bears engraved on its surface the name of King Herod himself, that would be the archaeologists' dream come true!

F OR DEVOUT JEWS THROUGHOUT THE WORLD, the northern
segment of the Western Wall holds the greatest significance.
It was one of the retaining walls of "the sacred House of God,"
Herod's magnificent second Temple. For Jews, this is the holiest
spot on earth. They believe it is the place closest to God in the
entire world.

Little is known about the origins of the Jews. Almost five thousand years ago, when Egypt, Sumer, and Akkad were building great empires, the earliest ancestors of the Jews were a tiny band of nomads wandering in the vastness of the Middle East's deserts. It is not certain what they called themselves. They threatened no one. They were not even noticed. They raised no grain or vegetable crops. Their food was the meat and milk of their sheep and goats. Where they found water and grazing for their beasts, they pitched tents and stayed a while. When the grazing grew sparse, they folded their tents and searched for new oases.

The Egyptian, Sumerian, and Akkadian empires surrounding those first Jews built monumental cities and commanded powerful armies. They had mastered agriculture, and their artistic achievements astonished the world. But they perceived that their powers were limited by the forces of nature. For them, the sun, the rains, the earth, and other natural forces were gods who had to be appealed to for protection and never angered. From clay, wood, stone, and gold, they fashioned imagined images of these gods, which they installed in elaborate temples and worshiped.

The Jews were equally dependent upon the forces of nature. But, as centuries passed, they began to wonder who or what it was that created all these forces. Eventually they began to ask, "Who created us? Why are we here?" It came to them that there could be only one Supreme Being who created the heavens, the earth, and all living creatures on it. The Jews called this God "Yahweh." Even though they could not see Him, they were convinced that He existed. This was a revolutionary idea and an extraordinary act of faith. To their neighbors, who worshiped many idols, the belief in a single, invisible deity would have been punishable by death.

No one knows when this conviction came to the ancient Jews. But according to the Old Testament, around 2,000 B.C., a dramatic event occurred. Yahweh appeared to a seventy-five-year-old man called Abraham, telling him that he would father a great nation to be named Israel. Yahweh proposed a covenant—a binding agreement— with Abraham. On the eighth day after birth, all male descendants of Abraham must be circumcised as visible proof of their devotion to Yahweh. If Abraham agreed, Yahweh would make them "His Chosen People" and deliver to them the land of Canaan.

Abraham accepted God's covenant. He crossed the Euphrates River into the promised land. For four hundred years, he and his descendants roamed as peaceful nomads in the land of Canaan, practicing circumcisions and worshiping their invisible God. They called themselves Hebrews, meaning "those who had crossed over."

Then, a terrible famine swept through Canaan. To escape starvation, Abraham's great-grandson, Joseph, led the Hebrews into Egypt where, for a time, they were warmly welcomed. But a cruel new Pharaoh came into power and enslaved them.

After more than three hundred years of slavery in Egypt, the Hebrews were led out of bondage by Moses, whose encounter with Yahweh would have tremendous impact not only on the Hebrews, but on the future of western civilization. When God gave Moses the Ten Commandments, He revealed his laws to humankind for the first time. Those laws, engraved on stone tablets by the Lord's own hand, were a blueprint for righteous conduct between people, and between man and his creator. While God had given man the freedom to obey or disobey his laws, He, in turn, would be free to hold men responsible for their actions.

For more than three thousand years, the Jews have struggled to follow God's moral and spiritual laws in the conduct of their lives. For more than three thousand years, they have clung stubbornly to their ancient traditions—for which they have paid a heavy price. Because of a complex combination of elements—their religious practices, their dress, their eating and social habits, their speech, their passionate fascination with ideas, and, above all, because of the widespread belief that it was they who were responsible for the death of Jesus—they have endured more oppression, persecution, violence, hatred, and prejudice than any people on earth.

They are not great in numbers. Of the more than six billion people who inhabit this planet, less than half of one percent are Jews. The miracle of their survival is founded upon an idea so powerful that, even today, in this modern age of science and technology, it is still accepted by most of the world—faith in a supreme God of infinite wisdom, love, and goodness.

Throughout its history, Jerusalem has been a city that attracted pilgrims. In March of A.D. 33, Jerusalem was overflowing with pilgrims from all parts of Palestine and other lands, who had come to celebrate the Festival of Passover. Among these was a devout young Jewish teacher and his disciples. Little was known about him until three years earlier, when he began to preach in the tiny villages and towns of the Galilee. He taught that all men were God's cherished children—Jews and non-Jews alike. He taught that God considered no man superior to another because of wealth, position, learning, or power. He taught that God's laws required of all men to express equal respect, compassion, and love toward one another, especially to those less fortunate than themselves. His words touched the hearts of those who heard them.

It was said that, through the spirit of God in him, this teacher had performed many miracles of curing the sick, the crippled, and the blind—that he had even raised the dead! Some called him the *Christos*, a Greek word for the long-awaited Messiah who the Jews believed would free them from their Roman tyrants. His Hebrew name was *Yeshua*—Jesus of Nazareth. Large crowds followed him wherever he spoke.

Jesus also preached against cruelty and injustice. In a time of increasing unrest and protest against Roman oppression, such preachings were dangerous.

Upon arriving in Jerusalem, Jesus went directly to the Temple to worship. Inside the Temple complex, he saw stalls where live pigeons were being sold to pilgrims for sacrificial offerings. He saw tables set up where foreign Jews could change their currencies for Palestinian shekels to purchase pigeons. Jesus grew furious to see such sacrilegious handling of money and commercial dealings on these sacred grounds. He strode among them, overturning birdcages and smashing the money-changers' tables. The Temple priests were outraged but, fearing to arouse tumult or riot in the huge crowds present, did not have Jesus arrested. Above all, they wanted no trouble with the Romans.

Three days later, as Jesus sat with his nervous disciples in an upper room in the city, sharing the Passover Eve supper, he announced that one of them would betray him. One among them would lead the authorities to Jesus and seal his fate.

What Jesus prophesied came to pass. Later that same night, he was arrested and imprisoned. What followed was destined to reshape the future of the world.

Today, in the Old City of Jerusalem, there stands a building that is the most sacred shrine for Christians in the world: the Church of the Holy Sepulchre. It encloses the place where Jesus is believed to have spent his last hours on earth.

CHRISTIANITY

Promptly at 4:00 P.M., an earsplitting, metallic clanging sounds from its roof. As a priest peers down, a solemn procession of Greek Orthodox monks walk toward the ancient building, led by a Turkish guard. At the entrance sits an old priest, blessing all who come.

The church is not simply a single building, but a hodgepodge of many chapels and altars joined, over the ages, by gloomy passages and stairways. It is dark and cold, the air heavy with incense and smoke from hundreds of candles.

The monks file into a large chapel, followed by nuns and the faithful. Richly robed, like a king upon his throne, sits the Greek Orthodox patriarch of Jerusalem, while sorrowful hymns are chanted in remembrance of the agony of the *Christos*.

Not far from where the patriarch sits, pilgrims mourn and pray where Jesus gave up his life. After much dispute, archaeologists are now inclined to agree that this may well be the original site of his Crucifixion.

The only accounts of what followed the arrest of Jesus are given in the four Gospels of the New Testament. But these were not written until forty to ninety years after his death. The Gospels relate that after being accused of blasphemy by the high priest of the Temple, Jesus was brought for judgment before Pontius Pilate, the Roman official in charge of Jerusalem. In consideration of the Passover Festival, Pilate is said to have asked a crowd of Jews beneath his balcony if he should spare Jesus. It is then stated that the Jews did not ask for the release of Jesus.

Historians disagree with theologians that Jesus and Pilate ever met. Pilate was known to be a cruel, impatient, and corrupt man, who would, most likely, not have wasted his time over the mere disposal of another troublemaking Jew. It is more probable, they argue, that Jesus was taken directly to the Roman garrison where he was convicted of treason against Rome and condemned to death. In the morning, after being flogged with iron-tipped thongs and mockingly crowned with thorns, he was forced to carry a huge, heavy wooden cross through the crowded streets of Jerusalem to the dreaded "place of the skull"—Golgotha, a small hillock outside the city's walls, where he was crucified as a common criminal. As he hung in agony, nailed to his cross, it was said that the heavens became black as night. Before he died, Jesus forgave his executioners. He was thirty-three years old.

After Jesus was taken down from the cross, his body was carried a short distance to the entrance of a small rock tomb, where He was laid on the ground, washed, and wrapped in a burial shroud. His body was placed in the tomb, and a huge round stone was rolled in front of its entrance to seal it.

According to the Gospels, on the Sunday after his death, some women went to pray at the tomb of Jesus. To their astonishment, the stone at the entrance had been rolled away, and the tomb was empty. But Jesus was seen forty days later in glorious form, ascending into heaven, surrounded by a host of angels!

After Jesus was crucified, his disciples fled from Jerusalem but returned to secretly continue his teachings. They came to be known as the "Messiah People," or Christians. They preached in constant fear of death at the hands of the Romans, who were determined to eradicate what they viewed as a threat to their authority. Eventually, some of the disciples left Palestine to carry the "Good News" of Jesus to the rest of the world, even to Rome itself. There, they were persecuted and slaughtered, but they clung to their faith and made many converts.

Over the next two centuries, Rome experienced serious internal problems. Political corruption and indecision left Rome open to repeated assaults by hordes of fierce barbarians, who swept through weakly defended outposts of the empire's northern provinces. By the beginning of the fourth century A.D., the mighty Roman Empire was crumbling into small, isolated pieces.

In A.D. 324, a new emperor, Constantine, assumed power. Surveying the chaos into which his empire had fallen, he decided to move his capital far from Italy to what is now Turkey. In A.D. 330, he began to build a great city on the site of an ancient Greek colony, Byzantium. He named it Constantinople after himself.

By then, Christianity was the fastest growing religion in the Roman Empire. Constantine's own mother, Queen Helena, had become a Christian and soon persuaded her son to convert as well. Helena then made a pilgrimage to Jerusalem, determined to find

the tomb of Jesus and the place of his Crucifixion. Constantine ordered the construction of a magnificent church to enclose the Holy Sepulchre. He ordered the construction of other churches as well. Jerusalem became a Christian city, controlled by Christians and barred to Jews. But Constantine's most significant act was to declare Christianity the official religion of the entire empire.

Christianity, which began as a small, obscure Jewish sect, had conquered the mightiest empire of the ancient world—Rome! The earliest followers of Jesus were, like their master, devout Jews who emphasized Jesus' teachings of love and compassion for all people. But, in the centuries following the death of Constantine, Christianity fashioned an empire of its own. In the name of Jesus, Christianity built gorgeous churches and cathedrals. Christianity acquired enormous wealth and political power, influencing and backing the ambitions of monarchs and their armies. In the name of Jesus, new worlds were conquered, whose heathen unbelievers were enslaved, tortured, and put to death, their civilizations destroyed, their lands and treasures confiscated.

During his brief life, Jesus was never impressed by wealth, political power, pomp, or dogma. Until the very moment of his death, he lived a daily life of unselfish perfection, leaving an example for all humankind to strive toward—if humankind cares to make the effort.

ISLAM

F ROM MINARETS HIGH ABOVE Jerusalem's Temple Mount, a haunting Arabic cry rends the air: "God is great! Come to prayer!"

Across the vast platform which long ago supported King Solomon's Temple, worshipers approach their great mosque, the Dome of the Rock. For Muslims, it is the third holiest place on earth after Mecca and Medina. It is the most magnificent building in all Jerusalem. Its great dome, covered in 24-karat gold, is a glowing magnet at the heart of the city. Its facade dazzles the eye with brilliant, hand-painted Persian tiles.

Muhammad grew up in Mecca in a time when desert and city Arab tribes constantly fought one another. Some Arabs were suspicious and superstitious and occasionally prayed to fearful demon gods. Their most impressive god was one they called Allah, meaning "the God," who, it was thought, might be the creator of the world and its people. Like the Jews, the Arabs believed that they too were the descendants of Abraham, the father of both races.

As Muhammad grew to manhood, he could not bear to see the vice and lawlessness practiced around him each day. He felt that men were created for a higher purpose.

One night, as Muhammad sat meditating in a mountain cave, an angel appeared and said to him, "Proclaim!" But Muhammad was frightened and protested that he was not a proclaimer. The angel grappled with him, saying finally, "Proclaim in the name of your Lord, Allah, who created!—Who teaches by the pen, teaches man what he knew not."

Its dimly lit interior is no less awesome, with its perfect marble-columned arches, stained-glass windows, and golden adornments. This mosque holds special significance for the followers of Islam. It also rests upon the original site of King Solomon's Temple.

Islam, after Christianity, is the second largest religion in the world. It attracts more new followers than the other major religions. Yet it is the least understood and most feared by the people of Europe and America.

Islam began with an astonishing man called Muhammad—the "highly praised." He was born around A.D. 570 in Mecca, the largest city of Arabia. When he was eight, he became an orphan and was forced to tend flocks of goats and sheep.

For the next three years, Muhammad went forth to preach the greatness of Allah among the citizens of Mecca. He was ridiculed, insulted, and persecuted, even threatened and jailed. After three years, for all his suffering, he converted only forty people. "Am I a prophet or a madman?" he wondered.

Over the next seven years, in a sequence of deep trances, the angel Gabriel came to him, commanding that he write, in the exact words of God Himself, his final instructions for how men should conduct their lives until the end of time. And Muhammad wrote the Koran, the Bible of Islam.

Unlike his countrymen, Muhammad did not believe in demons

or the power of stone idols. To him, the marvels of the earth and the heavens were visible proof of Allah's miracles. And the greatest miracle of all was the writing of the Koran by Muhammad. He had written it using perfect grammar and exquisite poetry. He who could scarcely write his own name!

Word of this miracle reached the city of Yathrib, 280 miles north of Mecca. A delegation was sent to Muhammad, pleading that he come to teach and rule their unruly citizens. By now, Muhammad had converted several hundred families to what he called the true faith. But the nobles of Mecca were outraged at his success, and were threatening to imprison him. Muhammad accepted the offer and secretly sent his followers before him to Yathrib. He and a close friend made the perilous journey at night with the armed police and soldiers of Mecca in hot pursuit. But Allah was with them, and they arrived safely.

Muhammad was appointed chief magistrate of Yathrib, general of its army, and its spiritual leader. He succeeded so well in meting out justice for all, in uniting its quarreling tribes, in turning its people's hearts toward Islam, that the city was renamed Medinat al-Nabi, the "City of the Prophet," later shortened to Medina. Tribesmen throughout Arabia came to see this "maker of miracles."

Eight years after his flight from Mecca, Muhammad had conquered not only that city of idol worshipers, but practically all of Arabia, with the sword and the faith of Islam, meaning "confident submission" to Allah.

Then, a mysterious event occurred. In a night vision, Muhammad was carried on his white steed, El Burak, to the center of the world, Jerusalem. He alighted upon the sacred rock on which Abraham had prepared to sacrifice his son, Isaac, as proof of his devotion to his God, Yahweh. Around him on the Temple Mount lay only the ruined stones of Herod's great Holy House of God. Muhammad was then lifted by the angel Gabriel to paradise, where he spoke with the prophets of Israel and received the final revelation of God's truth.

On his return to Medina, Muhammad described his extraordinary journey to its citizens. He instructed all Muslims in the land to bow in the direction of Jerusalem while praying. But when the Jewish priests and Christian monks of Medina rejected his tale as the ravings of "an ignorant fool and heretic," he ordered his followers to turn toward Mecca, the city of his birth, instead.

Still, Muhammad never preached against the religion of either the Jews or the Christians. He revered Noah, Abraham, Moses, and Jesus as great prophets. "Who but a madman could reject the religion of Abraham?" he asked. In fact, the Koran bears a strong resemblance to the Hebrew Bible and parts of the New Testament. However, while the Jews were convinced that God's laws applied exclusively to them and that the Gentiles, all those who were not Jews, were unclean, Islam recognized all men as children of God.

Muhammad did not believe that Jesus was the son of God. He also despised the Christian reverence for painted and carved images of saints and holy martyrs, which he called "idolatrous worship."

Idolaters or not, during Muhammad's lifetime, the Christians held complete control over the city he most revered, Jerusalem. The Byzantine Empire, begun by Constantine, was now solidly Christian. Jerusalem was established as the spiritual center of the world. The Church of the Holy Sepulchre drew pilgrims here from all parts of the empire. As for the Jews, those few who dared remain in the city, they were despised, cursed, and spat upon.

In A.D. 638, after months of siege, a huge Arab army marched triumphantly into Jerusalem. At its head was the caliph Umar, a devout Muslim. His first request was to be taken to the Temple Mount to pray. What he saw there horrified him. To show their contempt for the Jews, the Christians had used the mount as the city's garbage dump. On his hands and knees, the caliph Umar crawled through the filth toward the great rock that was sacred to both the Jews and Muslims, pressing his lips to its surface.

Fifty years later, a glorious mosque—the Dome of the Rock—was constructed to consecrate and enshrine the rock from which Muhammad rose to heaven. His footprints can still be seen embedded on the rock's surface. It is the same rock which served as a sacrificial altar for the ancient Temple of the Jews. More than twenty-five hundred years earlier, it was part of a threshing floor owned by a Jebusite woman who sold it to David, King of the Israelites, the exact place where he planned to house the Ark of the Covenant in the first great Temple of his new nation.

Muhammad died in A.D. 632. By the end of that century, Islam had spread far beyond Arabia and the Middle East, rivaling Christianity as a major religion. Under the banner of Islam, Arabian armies swept through the world and forged an empire even greater than Rome. It stretched from southern Europe, Spain, and North Africa on the west, through central Asia, and to the mountains of China in the east. Islam's spiritual, philosophical, mathematical, medical, and architectural explorations created oases of civilization and learning in the wake of its armies.

In A.D. 733, Islam's armies suffered a major defeat by the French, which drastically altered its course of world conquest. Had it not been for that defeat, most of today's world might well be Muslim. As it is, Islam has left an indelible imprint. Four of every five Muslims in the world are not Arab, but are citizens of many lands far from the Middle East, including America.

Some historians are convinced that Muhammad was the most influential man who ever lived. But Muhammad insisted that Islam's achievements were not his, they were God's. And this question remains: How could an illiterate goatherd have written, in flawless Arabic, one of the most widely read books in the world, the Koran?

Today, MODERN JERUSALEM is a sprawling metropolis that has spread far beyond the walls of the Old City, which contains the historic shrines most sacred to the Jews, Christians, and Muslims of the world. The majority of Jerusalemites are the Jewish Israelis who live mainly in the western part of the city, and in the ever-expanding suburbs and new settlements beyond its boundaries.

Once again, Jerusalem has become the spiritual and political capital of Israel, yet it remains a city divided. The eastern section is inhabited by the Palestinian Arabs. Few Jews venture there during the frequent outbursts of political tension between Jew and Arab.

Israelis put in a five-and-a-half-day workweek, which ends each Friday at noon. Then, the squares and broad walking streets of west Jerusalem are filled with people looking for relaxation and amusement. Street entertainers perform energetically for the passing crowds, hoping to attract shekels as well as applause.

Newly arrived Jews from Russia play soulful music nearby. Their future is filled with hope but uncertainty. Even for highly skilled Israelis, steady, well-paying jobs are scarce. On top of that, these immigrants must now learn the complicated Hebrew language if they wish to improve their chances of success.

Tables at sidewalk cafes are packed with Jews from all parts of the world, who are thrilled to be citizens of this holy city and of Israel, the only Jewish nation on earth. This afternoon, among these milling Israelis, even their customary impatience and sharp-tongued nature are absent. There is only laughter and animated conversation. Young lovers kiss, oblivious to the jostling of passersby.

Yet, amid the lively talk and laughter is a quiet undercurrent of nervous tension. At every intersection and corner, tough young Israeli soldiers stand with their fingers on the trigger-guards of their weapons, scanning the crowds for possible signs of trouble.

MODERN JERUSALEM

Friday is also the busiest day of the week at Mehane Yehuda, Jerusalem's biggest food market, where housewives shop for their families' Sabbath dinners.

Life is costly for Israelis. Almost everything they buy is at least twice the price of what Americans pay for the same items in the United States. And, while most Israelis earn enough for life's necessities, their incomes are heavily taxed in order to support Israel's expensive defense and social-aid programs.

Compared to her larger Arab neighbors, Israel is insignificant in size, measuring a mere 150 miles long by 50 miles wide. Her terrain is mostly desert and she possesses no valuable natural resources. As Golda Meir, one of Israel's late prime ministers, wryly observed, "Moses spent forty years looking for the promised land. So, why did he pick a place that has no oil?"

However, thanks to the small farms and kibbutzim scattered through this land, fresh fruits and vegetables are plentiful and within the budgets of housewives. On the other hand, meats, poultry, and fish, especially fish, are extremely expensive. Some housewives are not reluctant to voice their outrage over these prices. But what else is a wife and mother to do when she plans to prepare gefilte fish for her family's Sabbath meal?

Although Israel is now a Jewish state, the partition of Palestine by the United Nations has left Israel with an agonizing and bloody legacy. Palestinian Arabs have lived here since the seventh century. They consider this their land. But the Jews, whose ancient ancestors conquered this same land nearly fifteen hundred years earlier, have claimed it as rightfully theirs.

Today, hundreds of thousands of Palestinian Arabs live in crowded East Jerusalem; in tiny villages and towns nearby; in the West Bank, accessible by bus; and in the narrow, twisting streets of the Old City's Arab Quarter. Aside from those who operate buses, taxis, small shops, and food stalls, most Arab men earn very little money. If they can speak Hebrew and are lucky, their chief employment comes from the Israelis in West Jerusalem who employ them at minimum wages as day laborers, clerks, cooks, dishwashers, or room cleaners in their restaurants and hotels.

For Palestinians, the Arab Quarter of Jerusalem's Old City offers a haven of cultural reassurance. Its teeming markets and bazaars are filled with the aromas of exotic spices and foods, while sensuous Arabic music floats above the sounds of the bargaining crowds.

A merchant patiently reads his newspaper, knowing that before
long, his entire stock of freshly baked Arab breads will be sold.

A woman spreads newly picked vine leaves on the ground.
These will be bought, soaked in a brine of lemon juice, oil, and
spices, then wrapped around a stuffing of rice and pine nuts.

But no matter what their occupation, when the call to prayer is heard, the men who work here stop what they are doing and hurry to the stalls in the bazaar which serve as makeshift mosques. Here, after washing hands and feet, they bow toward Mecca. At this moment, the urgency of Islam is greater than that of commerce.

For many centuries, the Arabs and Jews of Palestine had lived side by side in peace, respectful of the other's customs and faith. But after the establishment of Israel as a Jewish nation in 1948, that condition swiftly deteriorated. The Israelis were now free to open their doors to the suffering and homeless Jews of Europe, the survivors of Hitler's Holocaust.

In the 1930s, the German Nazis under Hitler embarked on a campaign of horror and evil unmatched in human history. Their purpose was to eradicate all the Jews of Europe. They almost succeeded. Six million Jews perished in what has come to be known as the Holocaust. Today, so many years after that event, memories of the Holocaust haunt and hang like a shroud about the Jews of Israel, shaping their outlook and behavior toward others, as well as themselves.

Fleeing war-torn Europe, Jews came here by the hundreds of thousands. Israel needed to find new space for them in this tiny land. Most were sent as pioneers into the wilderness to build kibbutzim, to become farmers, to make the deserts bloom. But many of those new settlements were built on land long occupied by Palestinian Arabs. Violence and bloodshed quickly erupted between Arab and Jew.

In the decades since then, Israel has continued to build new Jewish settlements, not only in the Gaza Strip and the West Bank, but in the heart of East Jerusalem itself. Young Palestinian Arabs, burning with humiliation, frustration, and hatred toward the heavily armed Israeli soldiers who protect the settlers, have retaliated—some with stones, some with acts of suicidal terrorism.

In 1967, as the rest of the world looked on with shock and apprehension, the combined forces of Egypt, Jordan, and Syria launched an armed attack against Israel, determined to drive the Jews from the Middle East. To the world's astonishment, after only six days of brilliant military tactics, the Israelis emerged as the victors, dealing their enemies a humiliating defeat.

In Jerusalem, for the first time since its long control by the Jordanians, Jews could once more worship freely at the Western Wall. Bullet and shrapnel holes in the Old City remain as mute reminders of the desperate battle for its possession.

To ultra-Orthodox Jews and Israeli extremists that great victory reenforced their convictions that the ancient land of Israel—all of it—belonged to them by divine right. One need only look to the Bible for proof. Before long, they began to build new Jewish settlements in the Gaza Strip and the West Bank, where hundreds of thousands of Palestinian Arabs had moved after the partition of Palestine by the United Nations in 1947. To protect the Jewish settlers, units of Israeli soldiers came with them.

Israeli military police, without arrest warrants or civil trial, imprisoned, beat, and tortured whomever they suspected among the Palestinians of causing resistance or acts of terrorism against them. Some Palestinians decided that it was better to die while committing acts of vengeance against their oppressors, rather than live beneath their boots. Among certain Israeli civilians, the attitude toward their Arab countrymen was, "They smile in your face when they want something from you. But, if you turn your back, they'll put a knife in it."

Today, Jerusalem, the "city of peace," remains an unresolved enigma, not only for the Jews, Christians, and Muslims who lay fierce claim to it, but for the entire world. It is a city which rests upon a razor's edge. Nowhere is this more clearly seen than where the Dome of the Rock towers above the sacred Western Wall of the Jews. Many ultra-Orthodox Jews would like nothing better than for Israel to tear down the mosque and build a great new Temple in its place. If that were done, it might well plunge the world into a catastrophic conflict—and Israel knows it.

The Israelis have taken Jerusalem for their nation's capital city and spiritual center. They intend to keep it, "united," under Israel's rule. The Palestinians, after their struggles for independence, are equally determined to claim Jerusalem as their rightful capital, regardless of any other peace agreements made with the Israelis. The Christians, who are the smallest minority here, have no choice but to await an uncertain solution.

Throughout history, men have believed what has best suited them to believe. Personal gain and political advantage have seldom been distant from the worship of their various gods. But if God exists, whose God is He? Does He truly favor one group of humans above another? Over that question, terrible wars have been waged, and unspeakable atrocities committed.

As we travel though space and time on this lonely, lovely planet we call Earth, will we never agree to celebrate unity rather than division? Will we never agree that we are *all* related?